Praise for Peanuts For Christmas - The Epic Conclusion To The Trilogy

"I thought it would take another couple years minimum"

Poetry Week

"Conclusion? Promise?"

Californian Writers Coalition

"Groundbreaking! We figured it was safer to bury it deep."

Torrance Tribune

Praise for Peanuts For Christmas - Part Deux, The Sequel

"Rarely is a sequel as good as the original, but I didn't like the first one much either."

Torrance Tribune

"If we are lucky, it will be another 8 years before we see something like this again."

Poetry Week

" We waited 8 years for this? Really?"

The Poetry Society

Praise for Peanuts For Christmas

"It made me laugh, it made me cry, and feel really good about myself."

South Bay Writer's Circle

"The perfect Christmas gift!"

Judy Soper - Mom

"I am not sure I wanted insight into the writer's mind, but I got it."

Beach Cities Sentinal

Praise for John Schlegel

"I thought he was dead, and I am still not sure."

Publishers Tri-quarterly

"Schlegel must have spell check, he isn't smart enough to spell everything correctly."

West Coast Editors Society

"We are exceedingly happy that he moved to Torrance."

Hermosa Herald

"Some people were born to write, then there is John Schlegel."

The Underground Poet's Association

Peanuts For Christmas

&

Peanuts For Christmas
Part Deux - The Sequel

&

Peanuts For Christmas
An Epic Conclusion To The Trilogy

Poems

John Schlegel

John Schlegel
Xmas 2010

Peanuts For Christmas & Peanuts For Christmas Part Deux - The Sequel & Peanuts For Christmas - An Epic Conclusion To The Trilogy

Book cover design by John Schlegel

Author Photo by Steven Schlegel

ISBN: 978-0-557-75236-2

Published using Lulu - www.lulu.com

Printed by Sun Devil Digital at the ASU Bookstores

First Edition

Also By John Schlegel

My Poems Need Training Wheels

Dedication

To all of you who knew me before I was rich, famous, and not as good looking.

....

Acknowledgment

To anyone who knowingly or unknowingly provided inspiration for these monumental achievements. Also, to anyone who poured me a glass of wine or beer, and to Pepe le Pew and Wile E. Coyote, Super Genius.

Contents

Introduction

A little history on this collection. Peanuts For Christmas, the poem, was written about 20 years ago. The original Peanuts For Christmas collection was self published at Kinko's and given as a Christmas present in 2001. Over the years between then and the sequel I continued to write sporadically. Peanuts For Christmas Part Deux - The Sequel arrived on the scene in Winter 2009. You will notice an evolution in style between the two. All the poems in The Epic Conclusion To The Trilogy were written in 2010. Again you will notice evolution. I consider my style to be linear storytelling for the most part. Hopefully some of the stories will take you to a time and place in your life. Afterall, my poems may seem to be about me, but they are about you.

Peanuts For Christmas

A Collection Of Poetry

Peanuts For Christmas

My Aunt on my mom's side
gives me peanuts for Christmas
every year. Don't get me wrong
i don't mean a small gift, i mean
peanuts. The first year i had a choice,
but i told her i didn't like walnuts.
She must have it written down
somewhere. john gets peanuts
for Christmas. i've never eaten
any of these Christmas peanuts,
but they seem to disappear
anyway. i think she steals them
back when i'm diving
into the apple pie. She excuses
herself to help with the dishes,
but instead helps herself
to my stash of Christmas peanuts
and that's why i get them
every year. My sister once got
a sponge as a gift. No, i don't mind
getting peanuts for Christmas.

The Stripe

Remember Penelope,
that ever-so-shy
black pussycat
relentlessly pursued
by a loveable skunk,
one Pepe Le Pew?
What does it say
about this feline
that she couldn't see
past a simple stripe?
That, Mon Cheri,
makes you skunkish.

The Distance Between Us

The distance between us
measured in miles
is daunting and immense.
Stretching and reaching
toward you serves no end.

The distance between us
measured in smiles
is meager and insignificant
I close my eyes, smile
and our lips seem to touch.

Do me a favor
think of the smiles
and join me
in a kiss.

She

Blew through me
like a cool, cool
gentle breeze
and refreshed
my weary soul.
Her soft kiss
floats in my now,
not-so troubled mind.
Her taste lingers
on my wanting lips
and my every sense
hasn't recovered since.

The Midnight Moon

Walking under the midnight moon
my shadow following me as I go,
a lake-like ocean ebbs and flows.
While picking up flat stones to skip
or larger rounder ones for the splash
I make my way up the dark beach
to no exact place in particular.
Solitary thoughts lead the way.
I think of you and smile.
I think of you and cry.

Haiku

Red Spotted brown trout
rise to the yellow mayflies
behind rock eddies

Your smile infects me
your words haunt my weary soul
hearts mend too slowly

Your kiss left me wanting
the warm feeling of your lips
Loneliness prevails

deep breaths of cold air
exhilarate my senses
as did your kisses

The Rock

With as much grace as I can gather up,
I cast the tan hares ear nymph out
past a submerged boulder, hoping
it to be home for a red spotted brown.
As the weighted fly sinks, my attention
diverts to the bright yellow indicator.
With intense focus my eyes follow.
Nothing else exists at the moment.
Fluidly dancing in the current it moves,
a subtle hesitation sets my reflexes
into action, quickly flicking the rod tip.
Almost instantaneously the brown jumps
again and again with urgency and fury.
Darting upstream then down, he fights.
Slowly I begin drawing him toward me.
The battle continues until his energy gone.
I guide him head first into the net.
Leaving the net partially in the water
I dislodge the hares ear from his jaw,
and allow gentle section of the current
to take him. Momentarily he fins in place,
second by second gathering his strength,
until the red spotted brown swims slowly
to the far side of the submerged boulder,
the rock, that he still calls his home.
The perfect end to a sunny afternoon,
I cast no more, and make my way
to my rock, the place I call home.

Cheap Sunglasses

About two hours
into my drive from Denver
to Laramie I began to miss
my forgotten gunmetal grey
coyote polarized sunglasses.
The Conocco gas station
only stocked very cheap
non-polarized plastic versions,
but did have three-packs
of hostess cupcakes. I opted
for both, but soon
regretted each decision.

Today's the Day

Yesterday Wile E. Coyote
Almost caught the Road Runner.
The day before that too.

Today, undaunted he rises
refreshed and hopeful.
Drinking his morning cup
he studies the Acme catalog.
Today's the day, he thinks.

How does it feel
to be the Road Runner
relentlessly pursued
by a Super Genius?
Maybe you can tell me.
Today's the day, I think.

Demolition Derby

After the slick track race
the demolition derby began.
With fury, the nomad wagon,
nova, and camaro collide,
until one sputtering engined
beast crept weakly alone
amidst smoldering lifeless shells.

Sputtering, I creep.

77 Beers on Tap

Naja's on the pier
has 77 beers on tap.
You can't really count
the ciders, so actually 74.
Kara pours them for me.
She smiles as she does.
Her skin is satin smooth.
Somehow that makes
each beer taste better
and makes the mile walk
each way well worth it.

Anchor Porter

Heidi, Dave, and Jim
complained loudly
that the hot wings
were far too fiery to eat,
as I slowly sipped
my anchor porter.
Heidi reached out
and offered me the plate.
Savoring each bite I ate.
Open mouthed Dave and Jim
stared as I licked my lips.
After each fiery wing
I took a slow draw
of my dark anchor porter.

Mental Note

The mile walk to Naja's
for tall 20 ounce beers,
77 of them on tap,
isn't worth it on Tuesdays,
because Naja's is closed,
and Kara's satin skin
and tempting smile
aren't there either.

Christmas Gifts

I know people who return
unwanted Christmas gifts
to get the cash value instead.
I am left to wonder the thought.
How much was my heart worth?

The Kiss

Over and over
My mind recreates
that moment
when our lips
first met.
My heart rate
accelerates
at the thought
I realize I
could survive
on that feeling
alone.

Soaring

Standing on the tower
preparing to jump
with red cords attached
securely to my ankles
I first discovered
my fear of heights.
Yet while soaring
down through the air
I felt utterly
and completely alive.

The night we kissed
I soared again.

Something Wrong

There is something wrong
about sitting in a strange bed
in a cheap rundown motel
eating beef with snow peas,
fried rice, and egg flower soup,
cracking open the fortune cookie
and hoping it will come true.

Peanuts For Christmas
Part Deux - The Sequel

A Collection Of Poetry

Peanuts For Christmas – Part Deux, The Sequel

To make airplane conversation, a woman asked me
"What are you giving for Christmas this Year?"
There are many answers to this question.
I am partial to giving T-shirts with pithy sayings,
yoyo's or balsa wood airplanes because everyone
should get a toy to play with on Christmas,
Magic 8-Balls to prognosticate the coming year,
and holiday themed pez dispensers for the candy.
I thought of Christmas' past and my aunt Mary Jane
and her bag of Christmas cheer popped into my head.
She had inspired a collection of poems that made for
the greatest Christmas present that had ever been gifted.
"I am giving Peanuts for Christmas." I said with a smile.
She looked at me incredulously, "Your giving what?!"
I repeated myself. "I am giving Peanuts for Christmas."
For the rest of the flight we flew in complete silence.
Occasionally she gave be a very disgusted glance.
I then realized when giving Peanuts for Christmas
It is extremely important, maybe even vital, to enunciate.
It was not my fault, where was her mind anyway?
Everyone knows you give THAT for Valentines Day.

My Triumphs

Many have seen
me trip and fall
both in reality
and metaphorically.
Some have witnessed
me trapped in a bunker
where I lost
hope for escape.
My triumphs
for the most part
go unobserved,
but I'm fine with that.

Silver Oak

If sipping
a fine cabernet
with a beautiful,
charming woman
isn't heaven itself,
what is?

Elbert

Elbert is a strange name for a cat,
but that is the name my niece and nephew
saddled one of their cats with.
When I first met Elbert
he seemed feral, yet regal and spirited.
He wanted nothing to do with me.
I didn't take it personally,
and it didn't bother me.
The Elbert that lives today has changed.
Has a milky eye and his hair is falling out.
He might be blind,
but he can still locate me when I visit.
Unprovoked he finds my lap,
curls up to sleep, and purrs loudly.
He loves me, and I find it creepy.

I'm Not Gay

The slur came with a slur.
Too much holiday cheer
freed his mind and lips.
"Come on admit you're gay."
I looked at him in horror.
"My gaydar buzzes
when your around."
His raucous drunken voice
carried across the backyard.
"Come on just admit it"
No one at the party
missed the scene.
Would kissing the next
woman I spoke to
prove my masculinity?
His friends corralled him
and rustled him away.
I chose to pretend
the incident never happened.

No, I'm not gay,
but I'm not happy either.

Vanilla Bean Ice Cream

At the mention
of ice cream
with tiny bits
of vanilla bean
you shook
your hands
in excited
anticipation.

I smile and laugh.
Then I copy
your gestures,
knowing
all too well
the feeling.

Vanilla Bean
Ice Cream
doesn't have
the same effect
on me,
but your smile
does.

The Tide Came In

Our sand castle
was beautiful
until the tide
came in
and washed
us away.

THE ART OF BEING PERFECT

You might not have realized it,
but I'm... perfect.
Many of you might be saying
when I see a picture of John
perfect isn't the adjective
that pops to the top.

Am I speaking
of perfect Moments?
No, but I have my share
of those as well.
Times on the river
where I made the cast
to get the perfect float.
Instants where I said
the perfect thing to friend
when they needed a lift.

I am speaking
of the entire process
of being perfect.
Perfectly flawed,
perfectly inappropriate,
perfectly funny.

It took me years,
but I have perfected
the art of being me.
Perfectly me.

Stealing A Muse

My muse comes and goes,
but has been on an extended
holiday lately, leaving me
even more alone than usual.

In moments of desperation
occasionally I spring into action
like a superhero or in this case
a calculating evil antihero.

On Tuesday Coffee Cartel hosts
the Redondo Poets poetry reading.
I figured stealing a muse there
should be as quick and easy
as preparing top ramen noodles.

The first poet read passionately
of reunited lovers, but sadly enough
I have no former flames that I
desire to rekindle passion with,
more for their sake than mine,
so her muse would not be my type.

An ex con named bill spoke,
and frankly his muse scared
this white bread poet.

A fat guy read two free verse poems
one about turkey and gravy,
another on roast beef.
His muse would lead me to
an early cholesterol filled death.

The feature poetess reminded me

of my Grandma Leah.
I once stole her cigarettes,
but I would never be so low
as to steal her muse.

Then I began to think.
Did someone find my muse
to their liking, then steal
and hold her hostage.
Should I be out scavenging
the streets trying to rescue her?
Or did my muse find
another lover like you did?

Budget Crisis

Fiscal restraint calls
for hard decisions.
The governor thrashes
a dull machete
to hack through spending.
A scalpel might do better.

In our crisis
you cut with the precision
of a neurosurgeon.
I don't know
if the decision
was difficult,
or if a dull machete
could have felt any worse.

Taster Spoon

Each taste heavenly,
each bite delicious,
yet leaves me
wanting more.
A soft moan
of desire emanates
from deep inside.
Each spoonful
merely a hint
of what is to come.

With you,
I need a bigger spoon.

Two-Fifty Chip

After three consecutive 16's
that quickly turned into busts,
we stood up to leave the table
both with uncommon smiles.
With only a two-fifty chip
flipping between my fingers
I couldn't help but feel rich.

Sometimes 16 isn't a bad hand,
and as I continue to flip my chip
I know, it isn't the size of his stack
that makes a man rich.

Blind Spot

Traffic in LA is notorious.
In the hours spent gridlocked
On one of the assortment
Of numbers - 5, 91, 57, 110
Or the hell known as the 405,
Odds are that someone
is bound to find your blind spot.
If a collision doesn't ensue,
The blare of a horn,
Or a unique gesture does.

You found my blind spot,
The collision ensued,
And my entire world
Hasn't been the same since.

Psychic

With each flip of a card
my past and future lay
spread out before our eyes.

With each turn
I see you.
With each turn
she did not.

Thirty-five dollars
doesn't get much
of a psychic these days.

I Suppose

I am probably not the first
to find a trains'
rhythms soothing.
I suppose I am not the first
To awake three stops
Beyond my intention,
but I did find
the midnight walk
back to the Holiday Inn
cool and invigorating.

Playing The Odds

I took a quick draw of my Newcastle
as the cards hit the table one by one
until all nine of us had two cards
from the blue deck while auto shuffler
mixed the brown one into randomness.

The big blind next to me took a glimpse
of his hole cards as I mucked mine.
I know odds, and they were against me.
An ace may look nice, but in early position
with an off-suit 6 as a kicker, unplayable.

The bearded guy in seat 8 made it 10 to go.
A couple folds before the bookish tight guy
on the dealer button stacked 10 to call.
The small blind tossed his cards to the dealer.
As usual the headphone wearing man
next to me grumbled, but splashed the pot
with 8 more chips to protect his blind.

The dealer burned a card then flopped three.
Six, Six, Jack, as I tried to hide my disgust.
The grumbler checked while I took a sip.
The bearded guy tapped the table twice.
Bookish guy called out twenty, and stacked chips.
The grumbler muttered and pitched his cards
toward the dealer, the bearded guy did the same.

The dealer pushed the chips to the bookish guy,
and he stacked the his winnings and smiled.
I knew I had him beat, but played the percentages.
In the long run, I'd end up ahead in the game.
Hours later I cashed out for more than my buy.
The grumbler left without seeing the cashier.

I flipped the light switch in my empty condo,
And threw my keys and wallet onto the table.
I didn't bother with the lights in my bedroom.
My clothes fell to the floor and I slid into bed.

Would it always be to an empty room that I return?
I know odds. By now they are either insurmountable
Or entirely in my favor, but I don't know which.

Tee Ball

One year on Mother's Day
my sister caught a 9 iron
in the face while teaching
her 5 year old daughter
the finer points of golf etiquette.
One weekend my uncle duties
included taking Tabitha to T-Ball.
As she advanced through the sport,
the tee of t-ball disappeared,
and pitching began.
I was charged with pitching.
With each pitch, Tab would swing
and I would wince, fearing
that a projectile aluminum bat
would tomahawk my way.
Yet, Still I pitch,
because the wincing fear
is far outweighed by the delight
I get from her smile when she connects.

A Trip To Baggage Claim

Backpack in tow, wearily
I trudged down the jetway.
The wails of a small boy
greeted me as I entered
terminal one at LAX.
He cried like the world
was surely about to end.

By the time I reached
the baggage carousel
the boy giggle and laughed,
complete recovery at hand.

On days when life instigates
my slightly subdued wail.
My recovery takes longer
than a trip to baggage claim.
A smile, let alone a laugh,
might be days away,
and the world could be
at its end for weeks.

The Story of Cameron Mitchell

Cameron Mitchell was the smallest kid in the 5th grade at Chapman Elementary School. That was a big thing to me, because I was the second smallest. In my mind he served a great purpose. He was the most picked on 5th grader, and were he to leave his duties would fall to me. I never once picked on him, but occasionally laughed at the pranks of the taller kids. Along with being the shortest it was common kid knowledge that he was the poorest too. Cameron didn't smile much, but when he did I remember it being a good one.

On a Tuesday in October while on the way home from school applying shaving cream on his jacket was the prank of the day. I found it amusing, so I may have laughed as I road my bike passed. By the time I saw the shaving cream covered jacket flying my way it was too late. A second later it was lodged in the spokes and I was launched forward. Face first I crunched the ground. I popped up, as an adrenaline filled 10 year old. My fists flew at Little Cameron Mitchell repeatedly until an anonymous voice from the crowd cried out "Your teeth, they're gone!" Immediately the adrenalin filled fists ceased, and tears started. My feet decided to leave the bike and run home - straight to my mom and a mirror. This is where I found out the "Your teeth, they're gone!" comment was a slight exaggeration. Shattered would have been a better description.

From that moment on the afternoon is a blur. I emerged from Dr. Terao's office with silver caps. I don't remember smiling much for the next 6 months or ever speaking to Little Cameron Mitchell again, but I think I must have received a forced apology that was followed by a forced acceptance. I smiled more when I got my white plastic caps until they started to yellow. It's amazing how the seeds of self-doubt can grow from a smile, or lack of one.

I Still Haven't Found Her

It doesn't seem right,
but meeting the right woman
isn't easy in L.A..
At least for me its not.
With almost 10 million,
over half of them female,
I should have found her.
I've resorted to the internet,
more specifically Match.com.
I've responded to countless adds,
gone on many mediocre dates,
and a few promising ones too,
but I still haven't found her.

Then I saw the ad.
It was titled CuteNBald.
I may be 43, and my cute days
might be in the rear view mirror,
but there is no accounting for tastes,
maybe I would be the cute and bald
guy that she had long been searching for.

I clicked on the link for the ad.
To my surprise, she wasn't looking
for CuteNBald, she was bald,
and not by circumstance, by choice,
but it wasn't cute to me,
I guess double standards do exist.
Does my hypocrisy demonstrate
a lack of character inside?
It just might explain
why I still haven't found her.

The New Guy

To put it simply
I loved her
and needed her
to love me,
but I didn't think
I was the kind of man
that a woman like her
could fall in love with.

With an unseen cosmetic
I covered up my flaws
and character blemishes.
Yes, I loved her.
Too bad she didn't
love the new guy either.

The Candle

Uncle Danny knew
it had been a long,
sad, rough year for me.
As a Christmas gift
he gave me a burnt orange
candle with the Japanese
symbol for happiness on it.
On receiving the gift, I smiled.
On lighting the candle,
it became quickly apparent
that it takes more than
burnt orange wax, a wick,
a Japanese symbol, and a flame
to create happiness.

Over The Slippery Stones

Wading stick firmly held
in his upstream hand,
a nine foot fly rod in the other,
the old man slowly stepped
through the knee high current.
Crossing the slippery stones
he paused and looked toward
the riffle on the far bank.
A cutthroat rose to take
a small caddis as it bounced by.

After a few false casts
his deer hair fly floated
into the same riffle.
Once again the cutthroat
rose to take the fake fly,
only to find himself fighting
the old man and the current.
A brief battle ensued,
and ended with the tired cutt
landing in a black net.

As the old man unhooked
the colorfully marked fish,
I couldn't help but smile.
His weathered hands
lowered the cutt back into river
to swim back to the riffle.
Satisfied with his day,
The old man unfolded
The wading stick and slowly
Crossed the slippery stones.

At 38 I make my way

Across the slippery stones
with a bit more ease and grace.
In the old man, my father.
I see the rivers of my future.
I see a long black wading stick
and slippery stones slowing me down
I see my casts shortening just a bit
I see me becoming my old man
and there is nothing wrong with that.

Vietnamese Vermicelli

While I attempted to display
my skill, or lack there of,
with the plastic chop sticks,
you deftly maneuvered
one tasty tidbit after another.
I fumbled each and every
delicious morsel to my lips.
With each bite of vermicelli
and every passing moment
I feel my hunger grow,
knowing with certainty
it isn't the Vietnamese dish
that I crave, but the one sitting
directly in front of me.

Short game

Nestled in hills of Rancho Palos Verdes,
Los Verdes overlooks the Pacific Ocean.
Known for its spectacular scenic views,
but terribly slow rounds, I rarely play.
On the occasion that I find myself there,
my Mom and I are squeezing in the early nine.

As usual I am scuffling the ball around
with the worlds absolutely worst short game.
Chunked chips, bladed pitches, misread putts,
and miserable bunker play are common-place.
I mention to my Mom that I think hypnosis
by a sports psychologists is the cure I need.

Mom, being the one with a short game
honed by countless hours of shot making
and owner of not one, but two hole's-in-one,
scoffs at and dismisses the concept.
Practice until you can feel the shots
deep within your soul is the true cure.

I contemplate the idea, knowing I have
someone else living deep inside my soul.
I feel a melancholy wave crash over me.
A tear comes works its way out of my eye.
Maybe when she finds her way out of my soul
chips, pitches, putts, and bunker shots,
with practice, will be able to find their way in.

Peanuts For Christmas
An Epic Conclusion To The Trilogy

A Collection Of Poetry

Peanuts For Christmas - An Epic Conclusion To The Trilogy

For Christmas
I wanted
to give her
my heart.
She would
have preferred
a nice pair
of earrings.
I gave her
Peanuts
Instead,
thinking it
was like
giving a piece
of me.
Both of
my choices
were much
more, and less,
than she wanted,
and in her
eyes they
weren't returnable.

Photograph

My favorite photograph
of my Grandma Leah
is a black & white one
my father took.
It captures her.

He's probably snapped
hundreds of me
over the years,
yet I haven't seen
one that epitomizes
me completely
the way he caught
his mother.

That's more of a knock
on my life
than his photography.
Maybe one day
I will reach a point
to be captured,
but it hasn't
happened yet.

Baskets

She was the basket
I put every
egg I had In.
I'd hoarded my eggs
up to that point.
If eggs were a currency
she was now a mogul.
One day she decided
to make the world's
largest omelet.
Parts of me
laid cracked
and broken –
the rest consumed.
About then I lost
the taste for egg dishes.
A change of diet
became necessary.

It took me a while
but now I have eggs again.
I may even give
you one or two
to have over easy,
but the rest I keep
out of harms way
in the refrigerator.
Baskets, I've found,
aren't as safe
as they appear.

Forever Hollywood's Farewell To Summer

A thousand people, give or take,
sat on the cemetery grass
watching "The Night of the Living Dead,"
the now campy original version.
Laying on a blanket we sipped
an average cabernet from plastic cups.
Why I thought Greg Norman, the golfer,
would ferment a good wine is beyond me.
That is akin to thinking Carrot Top
would bake a delicious carrot cake.
I guess he might though, but Greg didn't.
I don't know if the two guys in front
of us were gay, but they were stoned
which made them entertaining,
and that's enough in my book.
The she on the blanket with me
thought we'd enjoy the movie
more if we were stoned too,
and asked me to ask the guys for a toke.
Usually a beautiful woman
can convince me to do almost anything
even if it's completely out of character,
but this time not so much. It lead,
to the first argument I ever had
in a cemetery. We kissed and made up
or out - another cemetery first for me.
A shot rang out and the last casualty
of the living dead, lay motionless.
A thousand people, give or take,
applauded on the cemetery grass,
and summer said its final farewell.
Later that night we kissed goodnight
and that was our final farewell too.

A Mere Five Minutes

I've read that we dream
every ninety minutes
throughout the night,
with each dream longer
than the previous one.
The first dream lasts
a mere five minutes;
the final one of the night
can take up to an hour.
My dreams used to be
unremarkable, forgettable,
and I'd find my pillow
without much anticipation.
Come morning I'd awake
without any memory
of my R.E.M. cycle.

A Santa Ana wind
blew her into my world
altering the significance
of my nighttime reverie.
Each dream improving
on the previous one
until the hour long finale.

I woke up one morning
when the grayist month
came and with it she left.
After that day I still
remembered my dreams.
They stood as mementos
of passed sunny days
during gloom filled ones.
I found myself longing

to dream the way I used to;
Unremarkably and forgettably.
I wished to find my pillow
without much anticipation.
I could make it through
a mere five minutes then,
but if she showed up
probably not the finale.

I'll Settle

If the studies are correct,
and the first dream of the night
is only five minutes long,
I'd better try to save you
for the final one which
is the hour long dream climax.
That's if my cholesterol
filled heart can take it.
Otherwise I'll settle for five.

Footholds

She managed to get a foothold
into my heart, but then again
I'm eminently climbable.
For me she was a sheer cliff
that I desired to scale, my Everest.
Skilled mountaineers commonly
perish on such expeditions,
and I being but a novice
foolishly climbed undaunted.

I constantly felt as if I
could plummet at any moment.
Fearless and exhilarated
I continued with my ascent.
At a crucial moment I lost
the foothold I thought I had in her
and in that instant gravity won.

My Identity

To some I'm the guy
that slips away, fly rod in hand
alone to meandering rivers
as an escape from the world.

To others I'm the sales rep
that seems to spend
more nights on the road
than I do in my own bed.

The golfing crew knows me
as the "mentally strong" one
that's uses beta blockers
to avoid panic attacks
with a wedge in hand.

To Tab and Quinn I'm the uncle
that is mediocre on the wii
but awesome at building
tinker toy structures.

On Tuesday's I'm the bald guy
that self deprecates himself to death
in prose, naked to the world
with mic in hand at the Coffee Cartel.

Tonight, we dance amongst close friends
and strangers. The question is,
who will I be to you,
and who will you be to me?

The Redcoat Is Coming

I date and love
like the Redcoats fought
during the revolutionary war-
in plain sight, sometimes on a knee.
You saw me marching
toward you from a distance.
My intentions were far too obvious
as I fired my word salvos,
one after another.
I guess you didn't find
any challenge in that, or in me,
because you quickly found cover.
Guerilla lovefare with its share
of subterfuge might have intrigued
you enough for another date or two,
but our Redcoat relationship
still wouldn't have survived.

Two Days On The River

Now that my dad
is 70, has lived through
multiple heart attacks,
has been given stints,
experienced angioplasty
and a triple bypass,
I treasure our time together,
but worry at the same time.

In Carbondale Colorado
I walked the banks
of the Sobris River
for an hour and a half
worrying the worst
until I found him
on a section of the stream
we hadn't discussed fishing.

I asked him how many fish
he thought I had caught
in the last hour and a half.
He said he had no idea.
Zero, I said, because I
had walked the whole area
we had planned on fishing
not once, but three times
not making a single cast.

After talking to him like
he was a five year old.
He apologized. Then said,
now you know how I felt
when you waded further
down the rapids than you

had intended to yesterday
on the Frying Pan River.
But he hadn't said a word
about his concerns then,
and I, the fool, did.
He apologized, but I didn't.

In A Nutshell

People ask me why
I am still single at 43.
I could explain it away
by saying I just
haven't found her yet
or saying I fear commitment.
Both would be lies.

This one statement
on a recent prospect
might give you a clear
picture of the situation.
I found her addiction to God,
and her probable belief
that my ultimate
destination would have
an extremely hot climate,
much more problematic
than her former addiction
and subsequent successful
nine month treatment
where she kicked her meth habit.

You see, I could say it isn't me,
but that would be a lie too.

My Mirage

She's nameless and faceless.
She's always slightly out of focus.
She's a constant mirage
on the horizon that keeps
me walking step after step
to drink in her cool water,
to kiss her with my parched lips,
to make use of those nearly
expired, yet optimistic condoms.
She's hope when I should
have none at this point.

The Spur

A seventy degree day
on the Provo River
with a small mayfly hatch
turned into a 35 degree
evening in Park City.
The night air chilled
my bald head more
than I had anticipated
prematurely ending
my tour of downtown.
People lose between
7 and 55% of their
body heat thru the head.
For me its definitely
toward the high side.
In need of constant warmth,
I headed indoors
and chose The Spur
for the live music
and a quick bite to eat.
The artist's self described
style of funk, folk, jam rock
included not one, but two
didgeridoo and what I
thought was an electric
violin, but turned out
to be a viola. Throw in
an acoustic guitar
and assorted percussion
instruments played barefoot,
and you end up with
funk, folk, jam rock, I guess.
Passion and soul flowed
from each instrument.

As I soaked in the music
I finished off another
cold bottle of New Castle.
A set or two later, I stepped
back into the night air,
but I didn't notice any chill.
The didgeridoo continued
to play on in my bald head
as I toured downtown.

Who Knew That Bleachers Sports Bar In Phoenix Had Satellite Wagering?

Kendall poured me
a Blue Moon from tap
and added an orange wedge.
At three seventy five a pint,
I considered myself fortunate.
I love watching the ponies
run live, but satellite wagering
holds very little appeal.
So, I focused on the Red Sox
Tampa Bay Rays game
even though I don't like
baseball much either
leaving the exacta's
trifecta's and quinella's
from Woodbine, Golden Gate,
and Del Mar to Donny,
who sat next to me,
the blonde woman sitting
at the corner of the bar,
and the bear of a man next to her.
As I watched another knuckleball
fly towards to the outfield pavilion
Donny accidentally put his son
on speaker phone while explaining
to him he had errands to run
and the neighbor would be taking
him to soccer practice.
The conversation ended
with "Love ya bud"
followed by "Love ya Dad."
Donny then ordered another round
of Bud Lights and tore up

another exacta ticket.
As Wakefield gave up
a third homerun, I paid my tab,
walked outside, called my dad,
and considered myself fortunate.

The Bar

Alright I know you
are thinking to yourself,
enough with the alcohol
related musings,
but that isn't the bar
I am speaking of
at the moment.
You are the bar
that I hold all others to,
and the reason Murray,
my favorite bartender,
is slowly pouring
another Guinness
from his tap,
so that I can either
strive to reach it
or settle and lower it.

Appetizer To A Hangover

I am good in small portions.
In sips or as a tapas plate.
As your first cocktail of the day
you found me to be very smooth
and I mix well with ice cubes.
As your hors d'oeuvre
the initial bite was delicious
but a spicy dipping sauce
still added a nice compliment.
Too much of me can cause
heartburn or a stomach ache.
I am the three day hangover
you don't want to revisit.
With you I have no sense
or desire to control my appetite.
I could eat or drink myself to death.
You came for seconds; I gave you
heartburn and a stomach ache.
On polishing off the bottle
I gave you a three day hangover
you don't want to revisit.

Counting Past Ten

My single
best punch ever
didn't compare
to the accidental
blow you delivered
to the point
of my chin.
Maybe one day
I will get up
from the canvas,
because you've
long since stopped
counting.

The Menu

Personally, I'm not one to brag,
but I make an excellent lasagna.
The key is the vodka cream sauce
and a layer of fresh spinach.
My meatloaf is almost as good.
The trick is using three kinds
of meat – veal, pork, and beef.
That and the pepper jack cheese.
My pad prik chicken is spicy,
because of the Thai chilis.
A little sweat appears when you dig in.
I recently made a chicken parmesan
that might even go over well in Italy ,
as would my hot Italian sausage sandwiches.
For dessert sugar coated lemon cookies
or a devils food chocolate cake
with a chocolate butter cream frosting
are what I consider my specialties.

I should probably expand my repertoire,
but I say when you are really good
at something, why mess with success?
Unfortunately, you got bored with the menu.

Inside My Head

Inside my head
you swim in
oceans of disappointment.

Inside my head
you navigate
an obstacle course of doubt.

Inside my head
you ride on
a roller coaster of excess emotion.

Inside my head
you run uphill
against winds of weariness.

Outside my head
you grow
tired of being inside my head.

Consequences

At an abnormally early age
I learned how to play bridge
instilling in me a card sense
that has come in handy ever since.
While playing crazy eight's
with my then current,
but now ex girlfriend
and my then 7 year old
nephew, Quinn, my ex
prematurely sensed victory
with two cards remaining.
Her bragadociousness
struck me as being slightly
over-the-top and unwarranted.
Clubs were in play, but I put down
an eight instead, changing the suit
to diamonds by saying "girl's best friend"
Quinn laughed as I explained the reference,
but I knew they wouldn't be a friend today.
My then current, but now ex girlfriend
asked why I was laughing too.
I said, "Draw, the whole deck is yours."
To that she said, "I'll get a diamond."
She figured out the futility in that hope
when I said, "Good luck with that."
"Then I'll get an eight."
I flashed that I was holding
the final eight, and laughed again.
Right about then my sister
entered the conversation.
"Tell me I didn't hear
that you are counting cards
in a game with a seven year old."
I'd have to deal with a disapproving

older sister as a consequence,
but Quinn and I still laughed
as my then current, but now ex girlfriend
drew the last card in the deck.
The consequences with her came soon too,
and then down the road they came again.
When instead of her drawing for a diamond,
I gave her one, she showed me
what futility of hope really was.
I guess I hadn't counted on that.

Notes

Page 1 — My Aunt Mary Jane now lives in Utah and since this poem was published I no longer get Peanuts For Christmas.

Page 2 — Pepe Le Pew and Penelope are Warner Bros. cartoon characters. Pepe being the coolest of the all.

Page 9 — Wile E. Coyote and the Road Runner are Looney Tunes cartoon characters. To this date Wile E. Coyote has still not caught the Roadrunner and neither have I.

Page 11& 13 — Kara no longer works at Naja's, I no longer live a mile away, and Naja's doesn't have John Courage on tap anymore.

Page 20 — Silver Oak Vineyards make a great Cabernet Sauvignon.

Page 21 — Elbert has since passed on. May he rest in peace on someone else's lap.

Page 26 — I can still be found at the Coffee Cartel most Tuesday nights.

Page 30 — I still have that pink $2.50 chip, and to me it is worth significantly more.

Page 38 — My front two teeth are now pretty white porcelain ones.

Page 41 — Occasionally I still light the happiness candle, and it still doesn't work.

Page 49 — Forever Hollywood shows movies on Saturday nights all summer on the cemetery grass.

Page 60 — Trevor Green is the artist referred to in this poem. His music has God-like qualities.

Page 64 — I have no idea where Murray is pouring these days.

LaVergne, TN USA
01 November 2010
202956LV00001BA/2/P